Laurence Yep

The Library of Author Biographies™

LAURENCE YEP

Katherine Lawrence

The Rosen Publishing Group, Inc., New York

For Dennis L. McKiernan, with many thanks and profound gratitude

Published in 2004 by The Rosen Publishing Group, Inc.
29 East 21st Street, New York, NY 10010

Library of Congress Cataloging-in-Publication Data

Lawrence, Katherine, 1978–
Laurence Yep/Katherine Lawrence.—1st ed.
    p. cm.—(The library of author biographies)
Summary: Discusses life and work of the popular children's author, including his writing process and methods, inspirations, a critical discussion of his books, biographical timeline, and awards.
Includes bibliographical references and index.
ISBN 0-8239-4527-8 (library binding)
1. Yep, Laurence—Juvenile literature. 2. Authors, American—20th century—Biography—Juvenile literature. 3. Young adult fiction—Authorship—Juvenile literature. 4. Chinese–Americans—Biography—Juvenile literature. [1. Yep, Laurence. 2. Authors, American. 3. Chinese Americans—Biography.]
I. Title. II. Series.
PS3575.E6Z78 2003
813'.54—dc21

                                                           2003011022

Manufactured in the United States of America

Table of Contents

Introduction: An Ordinary Life

Biographies of authors can often be intimidating. They make their subjects sound like people whose lives have been so extraordinary that for them, the usual advice of "write what you know" is easy because they have experienced so much.

For example, Jane Yolen not only wrote poems before she even started school, but as a teenager she took ballet lessons from one of the most famous prima ballerinas in the world, Maria Tallchief. Gary Paulsen has had so many outdoor adventures that his books are based on his own experiences, including eating squirrel entrails, grub worms, and rabbit brains. S. E. Hinton began writing the first draft of *The Outsiders* (1967) when she was fifteen, and it was accepted for publication on the day of her high school graduation.

Laurence Yep is different. His writing career proves that writing is more about how you look at life than how exciting your life has been. He was an ordinary kid who had asthma, wore glasses, and spent most of his spare time helping his parents in their neighborhood grocery store.

But while his life may have seemed normal, inside he felt like an alien who never fit in. As he expresses it,

> I was the Chinese American raised in a black neighborhood, a child who had been too American to fit into Chinatown and too Chinese to fit in elsewhere. I was the clumsy son of the athletic family, the grandson of a Chinese grandmother who spoke more of West Virginia than of China.[1]

Yep has used his own feelings of not fitting in to write books about "good, morally upright young people," who are in conflict with their parents. He says about his characters, "their conflicts do not force them to choose between right and wrong, but involve a searching for identity."[2] For example, in *Ribbons* (1996), *The Amah*

(1999), and *Angelfish* (2001), the heroines try to explain to their parents why ballet lessons are essential to life itself, and in *Later, Gator* (1995) and *Cockroach Cooties* (2000), the main character has to deal with an incomprehensible younger brother.

With nearly fifty books to his credit and multiple achievements, including a Newbery Honor for both *Dragonwings* (1975) and *Dragon's Gate* (1993), Laurence Yep proves that ordinary people can become extraordinary writers if they work at it. This is the tale of his journey from kid to acclaimed author, a path created by hard work and his ability to look at his own life and feelings with honesty and clarity.

1 Starting Point

Born in San Francisco on June 14, 1948, Laurence Yep didn't have the conventional childhood that was seen on television when he was a boy in the 1950s. In those days, all television families seemed to be white and middle class, like those on *Leave It to Beaver* (1957–1963) or *The Adventures of Ozzie and Harriet* (1952–1966). There were no Chinese families on the small screen, and the only jobs kids had on TV were paper routes or mowing the lawn. The only similarity between those lives and young Laurence's was having an older brother and two parents who loved him very much.

Chinese Place Names

In 2000, the process of converting Chinese characters into Romanized (European) characters (pinyin) was standardized. Based on Mandarin, the principle language of northern China, conversion to pinyin caused the spelling of place names to change. Peking became Beijing, for example, and Canton in the south became Guangzhou. The Chinese place names used in this book are the old names Laurence Yep grew up with and uses in his autobiography, *The Lost Garden*. The modern pinyin name is provided (in parentheses) for reference purposes.

The Family

Laurence's father, Yep Gim Lew (the Chinese traditionally put the family name first), was born in 1914 in the district of Toisan (Taishan), in the Kwangtung (Guangdong) province in China. Despite being born in China, his father had papers that said he was an American because he was the son of an American citizen. This was highly unusual, given immigration laws of the time, which made it very difficult for the Chinese to become citizens, and to this day Laurence isn't sure how it was managed. However, he suspects his grandfather's business partner, an Irishman named Herbert Dugan who owned a pharmacy, arranged things with the U.S. government on the Yep family's behalf.

When Gim was ten, his father brought him to San Francisco. Soon after his arrival, a photograph was taken. Laurence describes the photo of his father, saying:

> He is in pants that reach to his knees, called knickers, which most boys wore then; and he stares at the camera with a serious, frightened look, his hair cut short under his flat cap. He spent most of his first few months in America being beaten up by the white boys on the block; or when the white boys weren't around, by the one Chinese boy who wanted to beat up someone else for a change. However, my father had a certain athletic ability; and he soon learned American games and sports and used them to make his enemies into friends.[1]

Laurence's mother, Franche Lee, was born in Lima, Ohio, in 1915, the daughter of Sing Thin Lee from Yanping (Nanping), near Toisan. She grew up in West Virginia, first in Clarksburg and then in Bridgeport, with her brother, Davisson, and sisters, Mary, Susie, and Rachel. Yep's mother would tell tales of sledding in the winter and searching for Indian arrowheads in the nearby creeks. The family lived there until Yep's mother was ten, when they moved to San Francisco.

It was a difficult move for Franche. Yep describes the problems she encountered: "Beside the shock of moving from green hills to concrete ones, my mother also became the target of other children. She spoke both English and Chinese with a West Virginia twang. She also saw nothing wrong with playing basketball against the boys—much to the disgust of the old-time Chinese."[2]

Franche and Thomas, as Gim became known, met at Galileo High School where they were both athletes—Franche in track and basketball, Thomas in football. They eventually married and in 1939 had Laurence's older brother, also named Thomas (though few people called him that). When he was born, his hair stuck straight up, so they nicknamed him Spike.

During World War II, Laurence's father worked as a welder in the shipyards. By saving and borrowing money from family, he managed to buy a small corner grocery store (now a parking garage) in the Western Addition area of San Francisco, at the corner of Pierce and Eddy Streets. At that point in time, the neighborhood was a mix of white, Hispanic, black, and Asian working-class families.

The Second Son

Yep would later tell the story of how he was named:

> My brother was almost ten when I was born in 1948 on Flag Day, June 14—three days before my mother's birthday. In order to make him feel part of what was happening, my parents let him name me and he chose Laurence. It was only years later that I found out the reason why. He named me after a saint he had been studying in school—a saint that had died a particularly gruesome death by being roasted on a grill like a leg of lamb. (In fact, he is supposed to have joked to his executioners that they could turn him over because he was done on one side.)[3]

That was just the first of many opportunities for sibling torment between Spike and his little brother. On another occasion, when Spike, Laurence, and their family dog, Suzie, went for a walk, Suzie ran off in one direction, Laurence in the other. Spike chased after the dog, leaving Laurence on his own. Years later, Spike explained that it was the logical choice: Suzie ran faster than young Laurence.

For Laurence the feeling of being an alien started in these years. Looking back on that time in his life, he describes those feelings:

> Comparing myself to my athletic father, mother, and brother, I often felt like a changeling [a child exchanged for another], wondering how I wound up being born into the family. I felt not only inadequate but incomplete—like a puzzle with several key pieces missing.[4]

Learning Self-Discipline

The small grocery store his parents owned dominated the lives of everyone in the family. Many years later, Yep described the store's influence:

> A small grocery store is like a big beast that must be continually fed and cared for. Cans, packages, and bottles have to be put on shelves to take the place of things sold, produce like greens and celery have to be nursed along to keep them fresh as long as possible, and there are hundreds of other details that the customers never notice—unless they aren't

done. In a small, family-owned store, certain chores must be done at a specific time each day. There is no choice.[5]

Laurence helped in the store even before he was old enough to attend school. It was his job to "feed the beast,"[6] as he described the tasks of restocking the shelves and icebox, cutting up old boxes, and the other chores he did, including killing the cockroaches that would sometimes crawl into the empty soda bottles that were returned to the store for deposit. But even though the work was boring and repetitious, he later discovered that the daily routine he learned as a child helped when he became a writer. The chores gave a rhythm to his day.

There *were* treats, however. During the summer and in the slow early afternoons before kids got out of school, and before Laurence was old enough to go to school himself, his mother would take him on outings. Sometimes they'd end up at the petting zoo in Golden Gate Park, or the zoo, the aquarium, or the M. H. de Young Museum. His favorite place, however, was Ocean Beach, where he could go wading in the Pacific Ocean, build sand castles, or visit the amusement park, Playland at the Beach.

Even more important to Laurence than the actual trips in the car were the imaginary ones. In his head the family car became a stagecoach, a PT (patrol torpedo) boat, a rocket ship, or whatever other vehicle he would think of.

Isolation

Looking back on his childhood and wondering why he made the choices he did, Yep comments that he doesn't know if he "would have become a writer if [his] life had been allowed to follow a conventional, comfortable track."[7]

But when he was seven, everything changed. The government decided to build low-income housing in his neighborhood. To make room for the huge eleven- and twelve-story buildings, most of his friends' houses had to be bulldozed. His friends moved away, leaving him isolated and alone, and even the geography of the neighborhood changed. As he recalls, "In a matter of months, my old world was shattered as I watched the gray lifeless hills rise up over the streets."[8]

Like any kid, Laurence couldn't help wondering if he had done something wrong, and this was the punishment. With no friends left in the neighborhood, he had to learn to value games he could play by himself, putting his imagination to use more than ever.

Within two years of the initial destruction, the neighborhood had changed drastically. Though Laurence knew a large number of boys and girls who lived nearby—mainly because of the store— those were acquaintances he recognized by sight, not friends. If he wanted to play basketball or football, he had to go into Chinatown to see his school friends.

The sense of being alone deepened when he realized that to the boys and girls in the neighborhood, he represented all Asians, not just those from China, and they didn't see him as an ordinary kid. This idea was hammered home one day, when, while keeping an eye on a truck delivering groceries to the store, the local children, black and white, were pretending to be World War II soldiers. As Yep remembers it, they suddenly turned on him, making him a target. They had assumed he was Japanese. Laurence quickly figured out that it could just as easily have been the children playing at being soldiers in the Korean War with him as a North Korean. They didn't care who he really was, just that he was Asian.

Being Chinese

Being seen as a generic Asian and the enemy in children's games was a shock because Laurence grew up thinking that he was just as American as the other kids he knew. It hadn't mattered to his friends what his ethnic heritage was; they were simply all friends, all Americans. But when the children he grew up with were forced to move away, that feeling of being just another neighborhood child disappeared.

In fact, Laurence admits that back then he didn't really want to be Chinese. To be Chinese in San Francisco brought trouble, whether in Golden Gate Park when a group of white boys called him names and spat at him, or when threatened with a knife in a disagreement over whether he and his friends were allowed to play football in Washington Square, the heart of the Italian North Beach area.

In addition, he didn't like what he would later describe as the "artificial and commercial 'Asian-ness'"[9] of the store windows in Chinatown. Like his friends, he scorned the old ways, such as acupuncture, herbalism, and the martial arts. He did his best to show he was different from those who lived in Chinatown by insisting on using a fork, not chopsticks (he didn't learn to use chopsticks until he was twelve years old), and drinking Coca-Cola instead of Chinese tea.

When he was in the fourth grade at St. Mary's Grammar School, the nuns made Chinese part of the curriculum. Laurence went from being an A student in the English classes to being in the "dummies' class" because Chinese wasn't spoken at home. He didn't even know the basic words. Even worse were the calligraphy lessons.

He could have studied hard to catch up, but he didn't want to. As Yep now recalls:

> Resenting both the teacher and the situation, I went out of my way to pass the course but not learn Chinese. Each week, we had a new lesson in the reader that we were expected to memorize, recite aloud, and then write out. So each week, I memorized a new pattern of sounds like a song and a new pattern of pictures like a cartoon. I wound up doing more work than anyone else in that class but I achieved my purpose: I passed without learning Chinese.[10]

It was his grandmother Marie Lee who made sure he was aware of his heritage. Yep describes her influence by saying, "She represented a 'Chineseness' in my life that was as unmovable and unwanted as a mountain in your living room. Or rather it was like finding strange, new pieces to a puzzle that made the picture itself take a new, unwanted shape."[11]

In his grandmother's small studio apartment, there were small statues, incense, and Chinese opera record albums. She was fussy about her food, especially vegetables, insisting they be cooked just right. Because he didn't speak her dialect of Chinese (they taught a different one in school, so even if he'd learned it properly, he couldn't talk to her), she spoke English when the two of them were together. However, because her English was only slightly better than his Chinese, there were often communication problems. For example, though he wanted to know, he never asked her whom the statues represented because she wouldn't be able to explain it in English. All he knew was that they were important to her because of how she treated them.

Young Laurence didn't fit in well with his peers in Chinatown, either. Of the forty-five or so students in his class, he was one of the few who lived outside of Chinatown, in large part due to discrimination by landlords (which is now illegal), who rarely rented to Chinese outside of Chinatown.

Legalized Prejudice

Prior to April 11, 1968, when the Federal Fair Housing Act was passed in the United States Congress and signed into law, it was perfectly legal to refuse to rent or sell a house or apartment to people because of their ethnic heritage, a physical or mental disability, or any other reason. Landlords could indulge in their own preferences and prejudices and refuse to rent to anyone unlike them. Not all landlords did this; there have always been some who treated all people fairly, but they were rare. In 1968, however, prejudice of this sort became illegal. Everyone in the United States has the right to live anywhere they choose and can afford.

Laurence's lack of Chinese language skills was a problem at recess, too. His friends would tell dirty jokes in Chinese so the nuns wouldn't understand, but that meant Laurence didn't understand either, and his friends didn't bother explaining the jokes to him. What Chinese he eventually acquired was mostly insults learned on the playground.

2 Searching for Direction

In an attempt to find guidance for his confused life, Laurence became a Catholic, and then an altar boy. But it was the Chinatown branch of the public library that seemed to offer him the most hope of finding a solution to his problems, even if it was just escaping them for a few hours while reading about strange worlds and the lives of other children. Because his parents taught him that reading was a pleasure, he'd always liked books. They had one rule when it came to books: for each children's book or comic book they read to him, Laurence had to read one back to them.

Libraries

Among his favorite books were those of the Oz series, created by L. Frank Baum. Years later, Yep realized why he liked the books:

In the Oz books, you usually have some child taken out of his or her everyday world and taken to a new land where he or she must learn new customs and adjust to new people. There was no time for being stunned or for complaining. The children took in the situation and adapted . . . They dealt with the real mysteries of life—like finding yourself and your place in the world. And that was something I tried to do every day I got on and off the bus.[1]

Searching for all the Oz books led Laurence to the main library by city hall because that was the only branch that had them all. After the Oz books, Laurence discovered science fiction. The San Francisco library system marked all science fiction books with a blue rocket ship on the spine. In search of the rocket ship, he discovered the young adult books by Robert Heinlein, which he liked because the characters were funny and memorable. But it was author Andre Norton who was a special favorite. Laurence identified with the outlaws and outcasts that populated the exotic worlds and mysterious half-ruined cities she created.

In eighth grade, Laurence moved on to reading adult science fiction. He loved discussing the ideas and plots of books he'd read with friends. Unfortunately, that's when Laurence heard that one friend thought he was weird for liking science fiction. The books he loved reading had now become something that made him feel insecure and embarrassed. As a result, though he was scared to leave grammar school for high school at the end of that academic year, he looked forward to a chance to start over in new surroundings with new classmates.

Chemistry Vs. Writing

Laurence attended high school at St. Ignatius, a mostly white boys' high school where he was in the honors program. He discovered chemistry and earned extra credit by building explosives. For Laurence, chemistry was not only a responsible career choice, since chemists usually receive very good salaries, but it was fun. He planned to attend college, then spend the rest of his life working as a chemist for a large company. But during his senior year, those plans changed.

Laurence had an English composition teacher named Father Becker, a Jesuit priest who taught by having pupils write assignments in different forms, imitating various writers. For example, the boys had to write scenes imitating

Shakespeare. Father Becker took some of his best students aside, including Laurence, and told them that the only way to get an A in the course would be to have something accepted by a national magazine. Of course, Laurence and the others were intimidated by this demand, but as far as Laurence was concerned, one simply did not argue with a Jesuit priest. They tried to obey him—they wrote stories and submitted them, but nothing was accepted. Fortunately, Father Becker canceled the requirement and they were graded like all the others, but it changed Laurence's life. He later said, "I got bitten by the bug and kept on trying."[2] In fact, he discovered that making up stories was just as much fun as making explosives.

Writing, however, had benefits explosives couldn't match. As Yep would later write:

> When I wrote I went from being a puzzle to a puzzle solver. I could reach into the box of rags that was my soul and begin stitching them together. Moreover, I could try out different combinations to see which one pleased me the most. I could take these different elements, each of which belonged to something else, and dip them into my imagination where they were melted down and cast into new shapes so that they became uniquely mine.[3]

As a result of the joy he found in writing, Laurence was torn between choosing to major in English or chemistry in college. (Attending college was never a decision to be made—it was a given considering his parents' belief in the importance of education.)

Part of the curriculum at St. Ignatius included retreats, where the boys were led through several days of guided meditation. As seniors, the retreat would be away from the school for the first time, at a dormitory near St. Helena in California's wine country. But this retreat was different in another way as well; Laurence had decisions to make. He took long walks in the fields near the vineyards and slowly came to realize that he preferred writing to chemistry. Describing his decision years later, he said:

> "I think the sunshine and night sky also had something to do with my choice. Ironically, I decided that I didn't want to be locked up in a lab—little realizing how many sunny afternoons I would have to be stuck in my study because of a deadline on a story."[4]

Making Mistakes

Sensibly, he didn't expect to earn a living by writing fiction, so he worked out a plan. He'd try journalism first, and if that didn't work out, he'd teach English. He explained this to his parents and they gave him their full support. As a result, when his teachers recommended Laurence apply to the college of journalism at Marquette University in Milwaukee, Wisconsin, he did.

When he arrived there, the Marquette Laurence saw looked nothing like the one in the brochure he had seen. In 1966, the university was on an urban campus. Nearby hotels had been turned into dorms, and there were more homeless people living on the surrounding streets than there were trees. When the taxi driver dropped him off at his dorm, Laurence had to double-check the address. From the outside, it looked like a skid row flophouse. Inside, he saw it was furnished with well-used, Salvation Army–style furniture, nothing like what he'd expected. As far as he was concerned, "The only thing that separated it from a transient [street person] hotel was the bottle of emergency holy water on the second floor."[5] Then there was the fact that Milwaukee was flat—so flat that when a friend drove him off campus to see "the hill," which was so small compared to San Francisco's hills, Laurence felt like the car went over a bump. And Milwaukee was cold.

Though Laurence had been looking forward to seeing snow, it, too, was a disappointment. As he recalls,

The first time I saw the white specks in the air, I thought someone's furnace was working wrong and sending white ash into the air. It wasn't until more had fallen that I realized it was snow. However, it didn't stay fluffy and white but soon turned into a gray, ugly slush.[6]

Even worse was the ice. No one warned him about the ice and frozen slush that accompanies snow. The snow would fall, partially melt, then freeze overnight. The next day it would melt some more and refreeze. Aside from being cold, it was extremely hazardous for walking.

There were some good things, though, which he discovered over time. Most of his dormitory mates were friendly, and he made a number of good friends, including the editor of the university's literary magazine, Joanne Ryder, who was from Brooklyn, New York. It was Joanne who introduced Laurence to the Winnie the Pooh books, as well as C. S. Lewis's Narnia books and *Alice's Adventures in Wonderland* by Lewis Carroll.

However, not even Joanne could stop him from feeling homesick or from feeling alienated. At St. Ignatius, he was able to go home every afternoon and could visit Chinatown in the evenings and on weekends. However, at Marquette, he was isolated in a way he'd never been before—even worse than when he lost all his neighborhood friends at age seven. At least then he still had his family, Chinatown, and Chinese friends at school. In 1966, the extent of Milwaukee's Chinese community was one Chinese-owned laundromat and a Chinese restaurant. The situation on campus wasn't much better. Of the approximately 20,000 students attending Marquette, maybe 100 were non-white, and most of them seemed to be on the basketball team, so Laurence had nothing in common with them.

Also, journalism wasn't turning out to be a good choice. For the first time in his life, he received an F. His stories contained so many inaccuracies that one of his teachers suggested Laurence had more of a talent for fiction than fact. He began to feel he was wasting his parents' money.

Stuck in Milwaukee, only his imagination could take him back to San Francisco. That's when he finally decided to stop writing the contemporary realistic stories that were earning him nothing but one rejection slip after another. Instead, he would try writing science fiction.

3 Stepping Stones

Having decided to write science fiction, Yep sat down and wrote a story about San Francisco at a time when the city had fallen into the sea after an enormous earthquake. The hero of the story goes back to the ruins to try and discover his roots. However, it's also a story with a twist. Though the hero thinks he's human, he discovers he's an alien. Yep titled the story "The Selchey Kids" and submitted it to *Worlds of If,* one of the science fiction magazines he enjoyed reading. To his surprise, they bought it.

Short Stories

In 1968, after two years at Marquette University, Yep transferred to the University of

California, Santa Cruz. He planned on majoring in literature, but this time, he would be closer to home and lots of trees. Surrounded by redwoods and lying just north of the town of Santa Cruz near Monterey Bay, UC Santa Cruz, which overlooks the Pacific Ocean, is only 75 miles (121 kilometers) south of San Francisco. Visiting his family and experiencing the culture of Chinatown would again be part of his life.

While at Santa Cruz, Yep received word that "The Selchey Kids" was chosen to appear in the *World's Best Science Fiction of 1969*. It was quite an accomplishment for a first publication.

Over the next several years, while earning his bachelor of arts degree in literature from UC Santa Cruz (he graduated in 1970) and attending graduate school at the State University of New York (SUNY) at Buffalo, Yep continued writing and submitting stories, acquiring more rejection slips than acceptances. They weren't all nice rejection slips, either. One story was returned with the words "Who cares?" written across the top, and another story was rejected and the editor asked that Yep not submit any more stories to him. Meanwhile, he was selling some stories to science fiction anthologies such as *Quark 2* (1971) and *Protostars* (1971).

First Novel

During this same period, Yep was encouraged to try writing a novel. Three years after he sold his first story, his old friend from Marquette, Joanne Ryder, who was by then working in the children's department at the publishing house of Harper & Row (now HarperCollins), asked him to write something for children. He didn't complete the manuscript until he was in graduate school, but it was accepted, and Joanne was his editor. As a result, his first book, a science fiction novel called *Sweetwater*, was published in 1973. One reviewer stated that the book was action-packed and filled with exciting drama.

Sweetwater is a tale of a human boy and his family who are colonists on the planet Harmony. The surprising appearance of a native alien opens the boy's eyes to the reality of prejudice and gives him the courage to defend the most important thing in his life— his family.

The aliens in the novel are called Argans. Years later, Yep said, "At the time that I was creating the race, it felt somehow right to say that they were all uncles, nephews, and cousins;

but I couldn't say why it felt correct."[1] It wasn't until two years later, when he began writing *Dragonwings* (1975), set in Chinatown of the 1900s, that he finally understood why the Argans were all males, all related: they were based on his own ancestors. Due to the immigration laws prior to the 1960s, it was nearly impossible for a Chinese man to bring his wife and children with him to America. This resulted in China-town being filled with males: uncles, nephews, and cousins.

No Sophomore Slump

Yep's second novel, *Dragonwings*, was pub-lished in 1975, the same year that he was awarded his Ph.D. in American literature from SUNY Buffalo. Because he never expected to make a living from writing, Yep continued going to school after earning his bachelor of arts from UC Santa Cruz. He was planning a career as a college professor.

For graduate school, he had chosen SUNY at Buffalo even though he hated the cold. Buffalo was in New York, so he thought it would be easy to get to Manhattan. (He hadn't realized how far Buffalo was from New York City.) For the subject of his Ph.D. dissertation, he chose southern writer William Faulkner. When asked why, Yep replied:

> Because of all the writers of his time, he could never leave home. He tried all the strategies of his contemporaries by going to Europe, New York and New Orleans; but he always wound up returning home. His ties to Oxford, Mississippi, were similar to my own ties to California and San Francisco's Chinatown.[2]

Yep's love of Chinatown was the inspiration for *Dragonwings*. In the book, the protagonist, Moon Shadow, is eight years old when he sails from China to join Windrider, the father he's never met, in San Francisco. Windrider makes his living doing laundry but dreams of building a flying machine. As the story progresses, Moon Shadow grows to love and respect his father and believe in his wonderful dream. He even helps him achieve it. In order to make his dream come true, Windrider must endure the mockery of other Chinese, poverty, separation from his wife and country, and even the great San Francisco earthquake of 1906.

After acquiring his Ph.D., Yep intended to teach American literature, as he'd been trained to do, but even though he sent out 500 job applications, he couldn't find a teaching position.

Finally, he ended up back in California, teaching English composition and remedial English at different colleges, including Foothill College in Mountain View and San Jose City College, driving between schools to create a full-time workload with part-time jobs.

It was in California that he received some extremely good news: *Dragonwings* was chosen as a Newbery Honor Book. That was the motivation he needed; Yep decided to try to make a living as a full-time writer.

Published two years after *Dragonwings*, Yep's next novel, *Child of the Owl* (1977), was described by a reviewer in *Horn Book Magazine* as "a haunting piece of fiction."[3] The main character is a twelve-year-old girl named Casey Young, and the story is set in Chinatown in

The Newbery Medal

The Newbery Medal, the world's first children's book award, is presented annually by the American Library Association for the most distinguished American children's book published the previous year. Aside from the Newbery Medal, committees cite other books that are worthy of attention. These books are referred to as Newbery Honor Books.

1965. As described in the *St. James Guide to Young Adult Writers*:

> Yep writes for outsiders, or those who don't fit in. For Yep, this can mean being overweight, not being athletic, not being the perfect child—dilemmas faced by many young adults or at least ones they can relate to. Streetwise Casey, in *Child of the Owl* . . . learns, changes, and grows as she discovers more about her [Chinese] heritage.[4]

That same year, Yep published another science fiction novel, *Seademons*. It was followed two years later by *Sea Glass* (1979), his third book about being Chinese in America, which has been described as very thought-provoking.

Yep continued writing steadily, and in 1982, the first of four Dragon of the Lost Sea fantasies was published, *Dragon of the Lost Sea* (1982). The *ALAN Review* commented, "While action and delightful magic fill the pages, the strength of the tale is found in the unique characters and their interactions."[5] It didn't start out as a four-book series, however. When Yep described the writing process, he had this to say:

> I can never be sure where a story will take me. *Dragon of the Lost Sea* began as a

picture book in which the Monkey King captured a cruel spirit with a trick. However, I kept asking myself what had driven the spirit to her evil deeds in the first place so that the picture book finally grew into a conventional fantasy novel in which children from our ordinary world are taken into another universe. I had already done several complete drafts and thought I finally had a manuscript that was ready to be submitted; but toward the end of that version there was a special pair—a dragon and her boy—who stole the scene whenever they were on stage. I realized that I had to scrap what I had done and begin over again; and it's now taken me three more books to finish the story—*Dragon Steel*, *Dragon Cauldron*, and *Dragon War*.[6]

The reviews were excellent.

Grabbing Opportunity

Yep was now hitting his stride as a writer. He had three books published in 1982, another in 1983, two more in 1984, three in 1985, and one in 1986. One of the books published during this period was an odd departure for most Newbery Honor writers: a *Star Trek* book. Media tie-ins are generally considered by the literary establishment to be the lowest of the low, not proper literature at all since they're based on television shows or movies. But Yep's first love was science fiction, so one day he had lunch with New York editor David Hartwell, who was editing the *Trek* series. As Yep describes that meal:

> We actually talked over several possible novels; but then he said he was tired of all the [manuscripts] about Kirk and Spock. However, I then had "to prove myself worthy of entering the Star Trek universe"—to use the official Paramount phrase. I had to write about 40 pages about the characters. As I recall, I wrote a diplomatic reception scene. The [manuscript] also had to be approved not only by David but by Paramount and Gene Roddenberry [the creator of the original *Star Trek* television series].[7]

The end result of that lunch was *Star Trek No. 22: Shadow Lord* (1985), which features Lieutenant Sulu. It's original series *Trek*, with Captain Kirk and the USS *Enterprise* escorting a young alien prince, Prince Vikram, back to the alien's home planet after ten years of schooling in the Federation.

The themes common to Yep's books are clearly visible here. As Yep himself says:

> Probably the reason much of my writing has found its way to a teenage audience is that I'm always pursuing the theme of being an outsider—an alien—and many teenagers feel they're aliens. All of my books have dealt with the outsider—from the aliens of *Sweetwater* to alienated heroes such as the Chinese American aviator in *Dragonwings*.[8]

A personal preference of Yep's is also apparent in this book and, in retrospect, is there in all of his writing. Though the guest star—to use television terms—is a prince, it's the ordinary people, a servant and the servant's niece, who help the *Star Trek* characters (Mr. Spock and Lieutenant Sulu) save the prince's life when a traitor begins a vicious power struggle to gain the throne, murdering the king and Vikram's eight older brothers.

In his autobiography, *The Lost Garden*, Yep admits he has little patience with stories about rich and wealthy people: "Even before I began selling what I wrote, I was trying to tell stories about characters who survive at a basic level; and now when I look for folktales to tell, I usually look for stories about ordinary people rather than princes and princesses."[9]

Aside from being a *Star Trek* fan, Yep was also a fan of *Godzilla*, thanks to having seen the original theatrical release in the 1950s. Yep paid tribute to the character in his next science fiction novel, *Monster Makers, Inc.*, published in 1986. The protagonist in this book is a teenager who works for his father, a genetic engineer of small, theoretically useful animals. Among the animals his father has "created" is a very small (not quite three feet tall) Godzilla that escapes and accidentally terrorizes an expensive island resort. (Really he's just scared, but true to his genetic programming, fear can result in stomping things and/or spewing flames from his mouth.)

It was in this same time period that Yep had the opportunity to add computer games to his list of publications. He enjoyed playing them, so it seemed natural to write for them, and it gave him the chance to try something new. He's credited on two games, both adaptations of children's books, *Alice in Wonderland* and *The Jungle Book*, and both created for the Apple II and Commodore 64. He hasn't written for any games since then, but he enjoyed the experience and is open to the idea of doing another one.

A Personal Life

Books and computer games aside, in 1984, Laurence Yep married his college friend, editor, and fellow writer, Joanne Ryder. Yep describes their long-term relationship as being like the movie *When Harry Met Sally* (with Meg Ryan and Billy Crystal), with two friends who meet and separate and meet again, their lives intertwining over many years. Having met at Marquette University in the 1960s, Joanne and Laurence got married in San Francisco in 1985, and they are still together today.

4 The Golden Mountain

When Yep began writing *Dragonwings* in the early 1970s, he had no idea it would lead to an open-ended series of books. The original idea was to write a novel based on a real-life Chinese American aviator, but to write the story, Yep had to place the aviator in the proper setting—Chinatown in the 1900s. The setting of his book was similar to the Chinatown Yep had known as a child, where everyone knew one another. In the book, each character he created introduced him to other characters. Years later, while reading excerpts from the various books, Joanne, his wife, pointed out that because of all the interrelationships, he had a series about one family and its friends.

Today, there are nine books covering more than 150 years and seven generations that are part of the Golden Mountain Chronicles, named for the title the Chinese gave America: the Land of the Golden Mountain. While not written in any kind of historical sequence, here are the titles and the year each book uses for its setting:

The Serpent's Children, set in 1849
Mountain Light, set in 1855
Dragon's Gate, set in 1867
The Traitor, set in 1885
Dragonwings, set in 1903
The Red Warrior, set in 1939
Child of the Owl, set in 1965
Sea Glass, set in 1970
Thief of Hearts, set in 1995

In his introduction to the new editions of these books, Yep describes the relationship this family, the Youngs of Three Willows Village, has with America as an ongoing love affair, one that has lasted more than 150 years:

It has been my privilege to write about seven generations of the Young family and their friends, and how they have transformed the Golden Mountain and been transformed in turn. These books represent my version of

Chinese America—in its tears and its laughter, its hungers and its fears, and in all its hopes and dreams.[1]

Family Inspiration

Three of the books were directly inspired by his grandmother Marie Lee. In trying to imagine her as a teenager and a new bride, he created a character he named Cassia Young, who was a rebel in China during the nineteenth century and an ancestor of Casey Young of *Child of the Owl*. Later on, in *The Serpent's Children* (1984) and *Mountain Light* (1985), Yep tried to write about how she met the painful challenges of life and became the strong, unique person he knew as his grandmother.

Another family member, Yep's uncle Francis (born in China and married to Yep's aunt Rachel), helped with the research for another one of the Golden Mountain books, *Sea Glass* (1979), especially in terms of how characters spoke. Yep explains why he consulted with his uncle:

> I had had my fill of the fake wisdom that was put by American writers in the mouths of supposed Chinese masters—such as the master on the television series, 'Kung Fu.' The old-timers had learned a good many things; but

45

their lessons, like their manner of teaching, were likely to be rough-hewn.[2]

Inspired by History

The background of each book in the series reflects a part of America's history. In *Dragon's Gate*, the teenage protagonist, Otter, is forced to flee China after he accidentally kills one of the Manchus who governed the country in 1867. Otter comes to California and joins his father and uncle Foxfire in digging tunnels and laying track through the Sierra Nevada for the Central Pacific Railroad. The descriptions of the tunnels, from Otter's point of view, are extremely vivid:

> I didn't know what had happened to the light—whether the lanterns had all broken or the wicks had blown out—but it was pitch dark. Even at night outside, there's the moon and even if there isn't a moon, there's some faint light from the stars.
>
> However, inside the Tiger, there were tons of stones cutting us off from the light. It was a blackness that I could almost feel wrapping itself around us. Suddenly I wanted more than ever to get out of the tunnel.[3]

What's not mentioned, since the story is written from Otter's point of view, is that the

Tiger, the site of the most difficult tunnel of all, is the famous Donner Pass summit.

The most recent Golden Mountain book is *The Traitor*, published in 2003. The book is about the massacre of Chinese workers who were brought into the Wyoming Territory in the 1880s to replace striking coal miners. When asked about the events behind the story, Yep said:

> What struck me the most in my research were the few Americans who defied the mob and hid Chinese, including a woman named Grandma Williams. Their examples shine out like beacons of light so I wrote about a fictional family named the Purdys who befriend Otter, now the grown-up hero of *Dragon's Gate*, and his son, Joseph. In the *Chronicles*, it's not just the Young family who are courageous but the American friends they make in each generation.[4]

Yep doesn't limit himself only to tales of Chinese immigrants who came to California. With *Dream Soul* (2000), Yep wrote a tale of growing up Chinese in West Virginia in the 1920s. Called "a real winner!"[5] by *Library Talk*, it's a tale of the culture clash between fifteen-year-old Joan and her younger siblings, who long to accept their neighbor's invitation to a

Christmas party, and their parents, who think the children should be celebrating only Chinese holidays. With this book, Yep again uses his family's history as inspiration. As he says:

> I grew up on stories not only of China but of West Virginia, where my mother spent most of her childhood. In fact, I have two spiritual homelands—one to the west, across the Pacific, and one to the east, across the Mississippi. [*Dream Soul*] is a work of fiction, but many of the events are based on true incidents that happened to my family. Many of their stories are humorous on the surface, but there is a common thread beneath: that wonderful resiliency of the human spirit— that determination to sink roots into new soil and to flourish.[6]

So far, two of the Golden Mountain Chronicles have received major awards: *Dragonwings* was named a Newbery Honor Book in 1976, and *Dragon's Gate* was a Newbery Honor Book in 1994.

5 Today's Chinatown

After having several more books published in both the science fiction and historical fiction genres during the late 1980s and early 1990s, plus retellings of ancient Chinese and Mongolian folktales for younger children, Yep began writing stories about modern tweens and teens in today's San Francisco.

Sibling Tales

The first of these was *Later, Gator* (1995), a delightful tale of sibling rivalry inspired by an incident from Yep's childhood. In the book, after being reprimanded for giving his eight-year-old brother, Bobby, white socks for Christmas—a gift that their parents consider too practical—Teddy gives his little brother an extraordinary birthday present: a baby alligator. Teddy meant it to be obnoxious, but Bobby falls in love with the scaly reptile, to the despair of their parents and all the relatives who drop by to see what Teddy has done this time.

In Yep's own life, the alligator was a present he gave his big brother, Spike. As he recalls, "My brother was ten years older than I was so I could never get even with him. However, a pet alligator seemed like the ideal joke gift. I was that kind of child."[1]

Five years later, in 2000, another book featuring Teddy and Bobby was published, *Cockroach Cooties*. This time, Yep wrote about how Bobby and Teddy deal with the school bully, Arnie. As far as Teddy is concerned, "Bobby had to learn how to deal with problems on his own. Especially when problems were as big as Arnie."[2] However, when push comes to shove, or rather, when Arnie shoves Bobby, Teddy enforces a rule that pertains to big brothers everywhere: "Nobody [can] do serious damage to my little brother except me."[3]

To Teddy's surprise, it's little brother Bobby who discovers a lasting solution to the bully situation. Unlike Bobby, Arnie's scared of cockroaches. In fact, so is Teddy until Bobby helps him see what cool insects they are. With help from the neighborhood "bug lady," an entomologist, Bobby finds a way to engineer a permanent truce between him and Teddy, and Arnie. By the end of the book, Teddy has realized that his little brother isn't nearly as annoying as he'd believed. He says, "I know it sounds funny to say. But after years of living with a pest, I had finally found a brother."[4]

For Yep, the pet alligator is still a memory. Meanwhile, Yep's big brother, Spike, became an international award-winning physicist who mentored many others in Silicon Valley. He is now retired.

Ballet

Ballet is at the heart of the next group of books set in modern San Francisco: *Ribbons* (1996), *The Cook's Family* (1998), *The Amah* (1999), and *Angelfish* (2001). Yep's interest in ballet began shortly after *The Turning Point* received the Academy Award for Best Picture in 1978. He was asked to do a screenplay treatment (a story) for a ballet movie to be shot in China. The movie was never made, but Yep had what he considered interesting material from the interviews he'd conducted. Years later, he wrote a play about a woman with bound feet, and from that he made a connection between a

Foot Binding

In China, the practice of foot binding—breaking all the toes on a foot except for the large toe, then bending them under the sole of the foot and binding the foot tightly with cloth strips to keep the foot from growing longer than four inches (ten centimeters)—was done to girls before age three so the feet would resemble a three-inch golden lotus, which was considered beautiful and improved a girl's marriage opportunities. This practice seems to have begun during the latter Tang dynasty (AD 923–936). It was inspired by a king who found tiny wrapped feet attractive on a young woman. Other women then rushed to copy the fashion. Gradually, the situation became rather extreme. Foot binding was required of any Chinese women who wished to marry well and be respected. Peasant women who had to work in the fields and do a lot of walking were the only ones who avoided this fashion statement, but anyone looking at their unbound feet would know they were poor and lower class.

The result of foot binding was a lifetime of pain and the inability to walk more than a few tottering, unbalanced steps. It was banned by the Manchurians during the Qing dynasty (1644–1911), but the practice didn't entirely stop being done to girls until the formation of the People's Republic of China in 1949.

ballerina's misshapen feet (they get this way after wearing toe shoes) and the bound feet of a Chinese woman. Foot binding was practiced in China until 1949.

Linked through friendship and Madame Oblamov's ballet academy, *Ribbons* leads off the ballet series with Robin Lee's story. She's the eleven-year-old daughter of a Chinese American mother and white American father who love each other very much but don't always understand each other's cultures. When Robin's Chinese grandmother emigrates from Hong Kong, it creates jealousy and conflict among the entire family, especially when it means Robin, the star of her ballet class, cannot afford to continue lessons. It isn't until Robin understands why her grandmother is pleased that she isn't allowed to dance anymore that she and her grandmother are truly able to communicate and become friends.

In *The Cook's Family*, Yep writes of Robin and her grandmother's growing understanding of each other as they help a lonely cook by pretending for one afternoon a week to be the family he no longer has. Why he no longer has a family is part of the cultural history of Chinatown, and it provides Robin with a deepening awareness of what it means to be Chinese American.

In the third book, *The Amah*, the main character is twelve-year-old Amy Chin, one of Robin's closest friends and a fellow ballet student. In this book, too, the protagonist's love of ballet conflicts with pressures to stop taking lessons. In this case, the circumstances are different—Amy is needed to baby-sit her four younger siblings while her single mother works as an amah (a special kind of governess) for a wealthy San Francisco man and his young daughter, Stephanie, who is Amy's age.

When Amy's mother talks about how wonderful (polite and well-mannered) Stephanie is, Amy becomes jealous and their mother-daughter relationship becomes strained. A lot of hurt and anger occur before Amy realizes that sometimes the change you desire needs to come from within, and not by insisting that others change for you.

With the fourth book, *Angelfish*, Yep returns to Robin as the protagonist. She has just landed the role of Beauty in a ballet of *Beauty and the Beast* when she accidentally breaks the glass storefront of a pet-fish store. She doesn't dare ask her parents to pay for the cost of the large glass window; they can't afford it. Instead, she gathers her courage and offers to work there until the debt is paid off.

On television, everything would work out perfectly as soon as Robin took responsibility for her actions, but Yep is not willing to sum things up so easily. He parallels the rehearsals for the ballet with the relationship between Robin and the beastly Mr. Tsow, who manages the pet-fish store.

The Chinatown Mysteries

Yep next chose acting as a subject for a series of books and created the Chinatown Mysteries: *The Case of the Goblin Pearls* (1997), *The Case of the Lion Dance* (1998), and *The Case of the Firecrackers* (1999). Each book centers around twelve-year-old Lily Lew and her great aunt, Tiger Lil, a semi-retired but still famous Chinese American movie star who has played everything from maids to empresses and seems to know just about everyone in Hollywood.

Though Yep met Beulah Quo, one of Hollywood's most successful Asian American character actresses, Tiger Lil is primarily based on the actor Judi Nihei, who used to belong to an improvisation (improv) group in San Francisco, and who in turn was inspired by actress Eve Arden. (Eve Arden played Principal McGee in the movie *Grease*, plus a lifetime of other roles, starting in the 1930s with *Stage Door*, starring Katharine Hepburn.)

In the first book, *The Case of the Goblin Pearls*, Tiger Lil arrives from Beverly Hills and sweeps her namesake, Lily, up into an adventure, first as a dancing jar of Lion Salve in Chinatown's New Year parade, then as Tiger Lil's assistant as they search for the thief who stole the famous Goblin Pearls. The trail leads them through Chinatown to the operator of a sweatshop employing Chinese immigrant labor, and an insurance scam.

A lion dance competition between two martial arts schools to publicize the opening of a new restaurant starts off *The Case of the Lion Dance*. When the $2,000 cash prize that's supposed to go to charity explodes, only Lily and her aunt believe it was stolen, not burned up. While helping her aunt solve the mystery of the missing money, Lily is surprised to find out that her prejudice against immigrants who don't speak much, if any, English is returned by those who consider her "native-born, no brains"[5] or "hollow bamboo"[6] because she's too American and doesn't speak Chinese.

In the third Lily and Tiger Lil book, *The Case of the Firecrackers*, Lily gets the chance of a lifetime. Thanks to her aunt, she meets Clark Tom (the teenage heartthrob on the television show *East Meets West*) while he's filming an episode on location in Chinatown. When someone makes an attempt on Clark's life and Lily's brother is the primary suspect, Tiger Lil and Lily are immediately on the case.

Tracking down clues and interviewing witnesses, they visit a gang's headquarters in the Tenderloin district, a Chinatown social club, and finally a Chinese laundry where they prevent a second murder attempt. Of course Lily's brother is cleared, but the true winner of the day is Tiger Lil, who returns to television with a six-episode deal to costar as Clark Tom's aunt on the series.

Yep hasn't stopped exploring new settings in which to put characters and new media to write for, but he also does things other than writing.

6 New Directions

Though Laurence Yep will likely never stop writing novels, he expresses his passion for words in other ways as well. Unlike many writers and professors, Yep is convinced that writing is a craft you can teach someone. He says writing is "like building a well-made cabinet." He continues, referencing his years teaching at community colleges and universities,

> I saw a hunger in many students who were going to be computer programmers and physicists and scientists—a real hunger to express themselves. That's the part of teaching that I enjoy most. I especially enjoy the interaction—arguing with students who are so passionate

about things, for whom everything is so
black and white.[1]

New Audiences

In addition to teaching, Yep began speaking to
conferences and schools in 1975, talking about
writing and the Chinese American experience.
As a guest speaker, he talks to groups of 5 to 500,
from kindergarteners to adults. He also teaches
classes and workshops.

One often-quoted story takes place when he
was visiting a school to talk to the students. One
boy in the audience was especially difficult to
speak to—his body language seemed to say he
didn't care who Yep was, what he'd written, nor
about anything Yep had to say about China.
Using a technique learned from teaching
writing, Yep asked the students to imagine
themselves as alien monsters cast adrift in
modern society. The boy immediately started
paying attention and volunteered that he felt
like Godzilla. When asked to explain, he said
that it was because the monster was big and
clumsy and no one explained the rules to him.
That's why he broke things. That moment—
being able to connect with that student—is one
of Yep's cherished memories.

In smaller groups, Yep will sometimes assign a different kind of writing exercise. He says,

> I'll ask for a list of objects in the room. We'll choose one object—a lightbulb, say—and try to imagine it as a living creature. How would a lightbulb communicate with others? How would it get its food? We then try to imagine the creature's world. The last step is to make up a story about that world.[2]

Playwriting

Other kinds of writing opportunities presented themselves to Yep. In the mid-1980s, he was invited to be part of a playwriting experiment that included three science fiction writers (counting Yep) and three playwrights. Their goal was to create a science fiction piece that did not require special effects. He quickly became fascinated by the medium. "Writing for the theater was a real revelation to me," he says. "I can't watch someone reading my books, but I can watch an audience watching my plays."[3]

There were challenges to playwriting as well. Yep notes, "I know whether a written story is good or not by the time I've finished writing it. But with a play, I don't know until I've actually gone into the theater with the actors and heard the lines."[4]

His first big success was an adaptation of his book *Dragonwings*. The play was a collaborative effort between Yep and Asian American director Phyllis S. K. Look, and it has been produced at New York's Lincoln Center and the Kennedy Center in Washington, D.C., among many other places. Other plays include *Fairy Bones* and *Pay the Chinaman*.

Editing

A few years after that original playwriting invitation, Yep added another skill to his résumé. While teaching at the University of California, Berkeley, from 1987 to 1989, Yep realized there weren't any collections of stories by Asian Americans that he could use as textbooks for his classes. So he set about creating such an anthology, hunting down stories and carefully selecting excerpts from Asian American writers. Titled *American Dragons: Twenty-five Asian American Voices* (1993), the book is arranged in five sections according to theme, each accompanied by brief and eloquent commentaries written by the editor.

Whether he's paying forward, an idea noted by one of Yep's early influences, science fiction

Paying Forward

Long before the 2000 movie *Pay It Forward,* science fiction writer Robert A. Heinlein acknowledged in his books and life that none of us can ever pay back those who guided us and helped us as writers, and as human beings.

writer Robert A. Heinlein (see more about this in the box above), or learning new media with which to explore his craft, Yep's love of words and storytelling is always apparent.

7 The Writing Life

Writing is about more than putting words on paper—it's an art and a craft. There are elements of talent and luck involved, but most important, writing is about hard work: day after day of putting pen to paper, fingers to keyboard, and writing, like Laurence Yep has done. So, why do it if it is so hard, you may ask.

Yep has given this question some serious thought. He says he writes for children because, "you can get back to old-fashioned storytelling. Stories have to be told in concrete, vivid terms and relationships between characters are basic human bonds and therefore more universal."[1]

No Magic Tricks

Are there any shortcuts to being published? Any magic words? No. There is no secret hand-shake, no secret society that guarantees anything you write will sell. It's about working at the craft of writing.

Where do writers get their ideas? Yep says that writers never really know where their next idea for a story will come from. It could come from an old object, from a very small detail, or from something very simple—anything the writer reacts strongly to.

Sometimes it's not an object but something intangible, not physical at all, that inspires a writer. In an interview during a book tour to promote *The Traitor* (2003), Yep was asked to talk about his particular focus within the genre of historical fiction, why he chose it, and how it ties in with his personal experience. He responded by saying:

> The Chinatown I knew was very much like a small town where everyone knew everyone else. Trying to understand my parents and grandparents and that entire extended family led me to explore my roots as a Chinese American. Over the years, I've come to see that

there is a shape to Chinese American history that twists across time like a dragon uncoiling in the sky. And I've tried to capture that in *Dragonwings* and the other books of the *Golden Mountain Chronicles*.[2]

Crafting Characters

How does Laurence Yep create characters as memorable as fast-talking Tiger Lil of the Chinatown Mysteries or courageous young Otter of *Dragon's Gate*?

Working in his parents' grocery store as a child, Yep learned to listen to the customers and pay attention to them.

> I think I realized at an early age that what made people most interesting were their imperfections. "Their quirks were what made them unique and set them apart from everyone else. As a writer nowadays, I know that a character can come to life in a sentence if I can give him or her a "quirk"—whether it's the way they look or dress, some habitual gesture, or some favorite phrase—that makes them special.[3]

Research

Sometimes that quirk requires research, as do settings. But does research have to be boring?

Not to Yep: "Research is a lot like a treasure hunt for me," he says. "When I visit a city, I try to check out the library and local historical museum to see what either might have."[4] The real work comes in putting all that research to use. He continues, "Writing a novel is a bit like building a house of toothpicks; but before I can begin building, someone has scattered the toothpicks around the country and I have to pick them up one by one until I have enough to start."[5]

The Process

Once the research is done, Yep usually creates an outline, though he doesn't let it become a rigid taskmaster. "An outline is like the scaffolding around a ship you're building," he says. "You start out thinking you're building a cruise ship but halfway through you realize it ought to be an aircraft carrier so you tear the scaffolding down and set it up for the new ship."[6]

Even with an outline, writing a novel isn't fast; it's a long, slow process, like running a marathon. Yep states: "I know that I cannot reach the finish line that day. Instead, I have to be patient, trying to complete a shorter stretch of writing—a chapter for instance. I can only have faith that I will reach the end; and that belief keeps me plugging away for months to years to finish a draft of a novel—and a novel usually takes several drafts."[7]

Upon reflection, he thinks several drafts, on average, means seven sets of revisions before he's ready to show it to an editor. And then there are more revisions to be done after he receives the editor's comments.

Completing all those drafts, for each book, takes a considerable amount of self-discipline. For Yep, it's a matter of habit. Thanks to the discipline learned with daily chores at his parents' store, Yep is most comfortable when his days are shaped by a routine. He tries to write for four to six hours a day, and two more hours are devoted to note-taking and reading.

Though some writers use longhand and yellow pads and have someone else type the manuscript, Yep uses only a computer. He says his handwriting is so sloppy that his own mother has asked him to type his letters to her rather than try to write them by hand.

While working, he also listens to music. He knows he can finish a book when he has two things. The first is the right music. Using headphones to cut off outside noise and distractions, Yep plays the same piece or composer over and over again. For example, *Dragonwings* was written to the music of Ralph Vaughan Williams, one of Britain's greatest composers, who wrote everything from church hymns to symphonies before dying in 1958. *Sweetwater* was written to acclaimed American composer Aaron Copland's Concerto for Clarinet and String Orchestra. However, Yep doesn't just listen to classical music when writing. His two Mark Twain tales, *The Mark Twain Murders* (1982) and *The Tom Sawyer Fires* (1984), were written to the music of the rock 'n' roll group the B-52's.

The other thing Yep needs is a narrative voice. Each book has its own voice, a character's point of view that acts as a filter for the reader, revealing the story through that character's eyes and thoughts. For Yep, however, it goes beyond the writing into real life. He's able to settle into the character and become comfortable with him or her—an ability that can sometimes be challenging for his wife (depending on the nature of the character!). Ryder especially disliked what happened when Yep was writing the Dragon of the Lost Sea books, with Shimmer the dragon princess. Shimmer is opinionated, arrogant, and has a quick temper that sometimes makes it very difficult to be her friend. While writing her,

Yep admits the "dragon" in himself would also come out.

That's not the only difficulty in being married to a writer. In fact, both Yep and Ryder are writers, and both work at home. Because they both need privacy to work, their solution is to have separate studies. Due to varied deadlines, it would be very easy for them never to see each other, so they make an effort to share one meal every day, no matter whether it's breakfast, lunch, or dinner.

Aside from all the hard work, there are—of course—many wonderful things about being a writer. For Yep, "It's nice being able to daydream and to get paid for it."[8]

We should consider ourselves fortunate that Laurence Yep's daydreams illuminate not just life as a Chinese American—bridging those two worlds—but life as a human being in a society that seems to strive to alienate us from our fellow humans, turning us all into outsiders on our home planet.

Interview with Laurence Yep

KATHERINE LAWRENCE: You've mentioned that you like Godzilla. How old were you when you saw your first Godzilla movie? Do you have a favorite? If so, what makes it your favorite?

LAURENCE YEP: I saw it in the fifties in the original theatrical release in America. I think the one with his son [*Son of Godzilla* (1967)] is my favorite.

KATHERINE LAWRENCE: You've visited [West] Virginia, but since writing *The Lost Garden*, have you had occasion to visit China and see Kwangtung province, where your family came from?

LAURENCE YEP: No, but having worked on enough folklore from that area, I'm curious to see it. However, since the creation of industrial zones there, I'm not sure how much is left.

KATHERINE LAWRENCE: Do you collect anything? Do you have a particular pastime that you would like to share with your readers?

LAURENCE YEP: I loved Japanese anime. Unfortunately, so much of what is licensed here is driven by the testosterone market. There is some wonderful anime that emphasizes relationships and some fantasy stories, but I doubt if they'll ever be released here [in the United States].

KATHERINE LAWRENCE: Most of your books deal with alienation of some sort, but would you consider that the major theme in your writing? Do you view your work as theme-driven?

LAURENCE YEP: Actually, I think of my work as picture-driven. A book often begins with a scene in which I feel I'm simply describing a movie that has been projected onto an inner screen. All my books are about being an outsider in one form or another. If I wrote about an insider, content with his or her life, there would be no drama or story. We also live in a time of increasing alienation. We live in an age of irony and detachment and I see that filtering down even into the programming for children.

KATHERINE LAWRENCE: Have you ever watched *Jackie Chan Adventures* on either

71

Saturday mornings or weekday afternoons? How do you feel about the portrayal of certain aspects of Chinese culture in animation?

LAURENCE YEP: While I've enjoyed Jackie Chan's movies for a long time, I found it painful to watch his weekly cartoon show. The actors use that fake Asian accent and I can't stand the plots.

KATHERINE LAWRENCE: Who are your favorite authors—for young readers and for adults?

LAURENCE YEP: It's still a very old-fashioned list. I like Andre Norton, Robert Heinlein, and Rosemary Sutcliff.

KATHERINE LAWRENCE: Have any of your books been optioned for television or movies? Do you have one that you'd like to see on the screen?

LAURENCE YEP: Recently, Miramax has optioned my newest fantasy series, which begins with *The Tiger's Apprentice*, about a tiger wizard and the human boy who reluctantly becomes his apprentice.

KATHERINE LAWRENCE: What kind of fan letters do you receive?

LAURENCE YEP: They range from the generic classroom exercise where everyone copies the same questions from a board to some very insightful letters. There are also some very poignant ones.

KATHERINE LAWRENCE: Do you write every day? Do you have a specific room that you write in?

LAURENCE YEP: Yes, writing is such a part of me that it's like breathing, and I have a study. But when I used to teach creative writing at UC Berkeley, I used to tell my students to set aside a set time and place—even if it was only an hour at the kitchen table. Writing is like opening a window into your imagination and if you have a set time and place, sometimes the window opens automatically.

KATHERINE LAWRENCE: As an author, what impact do you hope to have on your readers?

LAURENCE YEP: I hope they learn that it's okay to be different as long as you are true to yourself.

KATHERINE LAWRENCE: Is there a question you've been surprised that you haven't been asked in an interview?

LAURENCE YEP: Well, no one's ever asked me what are my signs. I'm a Gemini by Western tradition and a rat according to the Chinese zodiac.

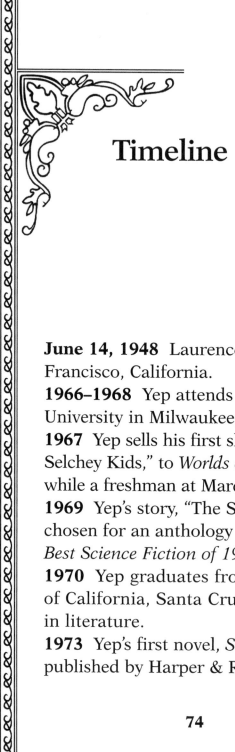

Timeline

June 14, 1948 Laurence Yep is born in San Francisco, California.

1966–1968 Yep attends Marquette University in Milwaukee, Wisconsin.

1967 Yep sells his first short story, "The Selchey Kids," to *Worlds of If* at age eighteen, while a freshman at Marquette University.

1969 Yep's story, "The Selchey Kids," is chosen for an anthology collection, *World's Best Science Fiction of 1969*.

1970 Yep graduates from the University of California, Santa Cruz, with a B.A. in literature.

1973 Yep's first novel, *Sweetwater*, is published by Harper & Row.

1975 Yep graduates from the State University of New York at Buffalo, with a Ph.D. in English literature.

1975 *Dragonwings* is published by Harper & Row Children's Books.

1975 Yep is a part-time instructor of English at Foothill College, in Mountain View, California.

1975–1976 Yep is a creative writing instructor at San Jose City College, California.

1976 *Dragonwings* is chosen as a Newbery Honor Book.

1985 Yep marries Joanne Ryder in San Francisco.

1987–1989 Yep is a lecturer in Asian American studies at the University of California, Berkeley.

1990 Yep is a writer-in-residence at the University of California, Santa Barbara.

1990 Yep is awarded a National Endowment for the Arts fellowship in fiction.

1994 *Dragon's Gate* is chosen as a Newbery Honor Book.

2003 Miramax acquires film rights to *The Tiger's Apprentice* trilogy, published by HarperCollins Children's Books.

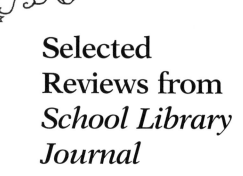

Selected Reviews from *School Library Journal*

Angelfish
June 2001

Gr 5–8—An appealing sequel to *Ribbons* (1996) and *The Cook's Family* (1998, both Putnam). Robin has just won the plum role of Beauty in the Beauty and the Beast segment of her San Francisco dance school's production of Ravel's *Mother Goose Suite*. As she and her friends are leaving the school, she playfully tosses her book bag at one of them and it goes through the plate-glass window of a pet store. The manager comes storming out, and Robin offers to work for him until the window is paid off. At first, he is rude to her because she is a "bunhead," and then because she is only half-Chinese. The relationship between Robin and Mr. Tsow parallels the relationship between Beauty and the Beast, as the girl slowly comes to discover that he is not the monster he pretends to be. Eventually, she discovers that he was the most famous dancer in China until the Cultural Revolution, when his toes were cut off as punishment for his "crimes." When the woman who is supposed to design the costumes and sets for the production suddenly leaves, Robin convinces Mr. Tsow to take over. The conclusion is a bit pat, but Yep does offer some insightful and amusing insights into the life of a young Chinese American as well as some historical facts about the Chinese Cultural Revolution. An entertaining read with an engaging and resourceful protagonist.

The Case of the Goblin Pearls
December 1996

Yep . . . is off to a roaring start with this launch to a mystery series set in San Francisco's Chinatown. As it begins, twelve-year-old Lily's glamorous great-aunt ("Tiger Lil") comes to visit from Hollywood. A whirlwind of energy, the sixty-something former film star ropes Lily and her family and friends into helping with a float she's been hired to organize for the Chinese New Year parade. In the process, Lily learns a great deal about her personal and cultural heritage, and she and her "auntie" help unravel an insurance scam involving a stolen pearl necklace, as well as uncover a sweatshop operation at which the mother of one of Lily's school friends is haplessly employed. Snappy dialogue, realistic characterizations and a plot with lots of action keep the pages turning, and the layers of social relevance (the sweatshop story line; Lily's growing realization of the complexities of her Chinese heritage) add substance. Readers will look forward to more installments featuring this spunky heroine—not to mention her wise-cracking auntie.

The Case of the Lion Dance
1998
Gr 4–7—Tiger Lil and her niece, Lily, first introduced in *The Case of the Goblin Pearls* (HarperCollins, 1997), are back. As part of the festivities for the opening of her friends' new restaurant, Auntie has invited students from two local martial-arts schools to compete in a Lion Dance contest. Kong, one of the competitors, is an angry, native-born Chinese teen who has no patience for Lily, who was born in the U.S. and

speaks Chinese only haltingly. He has even less respect for Barry Fisher, the other contestant and the son of the restaurant owners. His mother is of Chinese descent, but his father is not. At the conclusion of the competition, an explosion injures both Barry and his brother. In addition, $2000 has been stolen, and sore loser Kong appears to be a prime suspect. Although prejudiced himself, Kong's teacher instructs his reluctant pupil to assist Auntie Lil and Lily in finding the thief. Yep does a fine job of weaving in lessons on Chinese culture and life in San Francisco's Chinatown as well as the need for racial and ethnic tolerance. As Lily and Kong work together to solve the crime, she begins to understand what lies behind his arrogance and anger. Kong also finds that he has misjudged Lily. Yep's style is entertaining, and the pace of the story moves quickly enough to sustain interest. Fans of lighthearted mysteries will enjoy this book.

Dragon War
1992

Gr 6 Up—The evil, immortal, Boneless King, inhabiting the body of the human tyrant, Butcher, has declared all-out war on dragonkind. In this concluding volume in the series, Shimmer, the dragon princess, and her friends join her beleaguered kin as they fight for their lives. Monkey, an ebullient trickster-hero from Chinese folklore, recounts harrowing captures; hairsbreadth escapes; clever ruses; vast battles on air, land, and sea; heroic sacrifices; and dizzying, sometimes confusing, shape changes. Thorn, the human boy who has been Shimmer's companion since *Dragon of the Lost Sea* (1982), who helped her regain the magic cauldron in *Dragon Steel* (1985), and who sacrificed his body to reforge the cauldron in *Dragon Cauldron* (1991, all HarperCollins), spends most of this book as the soul of the cauldron, an object of enormous power. With the help of some potent immortals, both Thorn and Shimmer regain their rightful heritage. While the swirl of inventive details may obscure the emotional trajectory, the story provides a rare glimpse of Chinese mythic patterns. Shimmer's adventures continue to emphasize group loyalty over personal honor, and conclude with an audacious scene portraying the "many worlds of which ours is only one possibility," a concept rooted in Taoist and Buddhist thought. Because it would be hard to follow events and character changes without reading the earlier books, this one is recommended where the others have been enjoyed.

Dream Soul
October 2000

Gr 4–8—As the eldest child of stern Chinese immigrant parents, fifteen-year-old Joanie Lee is held strictly accountable for her high-spirited younger siblings. Expected to master her American school lessons and assist in the family's laborious post–World War I laundry, Joanie finds that her life brightens when their landlady wrings a promise to celebrate Christmas from the reluctant Mr. Lee, who adds the provision that the children must be perfect during the remaining weeks, a seemingly impossible task. Recent arrivals, the aristocratic Victoria Barrington and her charming father, provide some fun and friendship. Problems arise, however, when long workdays and the cold West Virginia winter make the scholarly Mr. Lee seriously ill. Facing the crisis with what she once passively rejected, Joanie fuses the wisdom of Chinese folklore with her own American grit to find her way. Details of landscape, climate, and period are quite evocative. Major characters are fully developed. Even the minor figures are interesting. Joanie's evolution in understanding the strength, love, and culture with which her parents have always graced her is warming. Although the cultural contrasts between East and West are reminiscent of Linda Crew's *Children of the River* (Laurel Leaf, 1991), Yep's lovingly crafted offering is for younger readers and has its own wonderful perspective.

The Journal of Wong Ming-Chung: A Chinese Miner, California
April 2000
Gr 5–8—Through his diary, a twelve-year-old Chinese boy nicknamed "Runt" shares his thoughts, fears, insecurities, and adventures. When Runt's older brother, Blessing, is summoned to California by his uncle, his parents choose to send their younger son instead. Runt learns the hard way that although the Golden Mountain brings the promise of prosperity to his family in China, it also brings hardship, racism, and even death to the "guests" mining for gold. Despite the many difficulties that he is exposed to, however, Runt always has a positive outlook on life. The engrossing story involves readers from start to finish. Yep deals with timely issues, including racism, bullying, and trying to find self-worth. A historical note about the Gold Rush and

black-and-white photos and illustrations of actual Chinese miners are appended. An engaging book with strong characters that successfully weaves fact with fiction.

Later, Gator
May 1995

Adopting a light tone far removed from the solemnity of Hiroshima . . . Yep trains his attention on a close-knit family in San Francisco's Chinatown. Teddy's mother, insisting that he put some effort into choosing a birthday present for his practically perfect younger brother, sends him to the pet shop to buy a turtle. But Teddy, no paragon, picks out a baby alligator instead, hoping to horrify little Bobby. (A note tacked onto the end of the novel advises readers on more humane approaches to choosing a pet.) Bobby, however, is thrilled, and Teddy finds himself working with Bobby to persuade their parents to let the alligator stay. Yep's portrayal of the family is warm, wise and humorous. In examining classic issues like sibling rivalry, he adds the special filter of the Chinese American experience: just after Teddy complains to his mother that everyone likes Bobby better than him, Teddy tells the reader,

"Right about now I could have really used a hug. My parents, though, never showed their affection like the white parents on television. I wanted a hug so bad that it almost hurt." The story may be a slender one, but the insights here are generous.

The Rainbow People
May 1989

The sections into which these twenty stories are grouped—"Tricksters," "Fools," "Virtues and Vices," "In Chinese-America" and "Love"—offer readers a way to pick and choose their ways through the stories. But the best way to read this book is in one gulp, treasuring each bite of wisdom and wit Yep offers. The stories are as much about common sense and kind hearts as about enchantment and unearthly beings. In "The Child of Calamity," an old woman finally makes peace with her own bad luck; in "The Professor of Smells," an avowed gambler makes a bet on the limits of his own good luck—and wins. Yep introduces the collection by recalling the works of early Chinese-Americans, and the ways in which these tales reflected or instructed those lives. With or without this knowledge, this is a collection that will enlighten and beguile. Ages 8–12.

The Star Fisher
May 1991

Fifteen-year-old Joan Lee tells of her family's hard-won acceptance as the first Chinese-Americans in a small West Virginia town. It is 1927, and few in Clarksburg have the breadth of experience or spirit to offer foreigners their friendship. The Lees are greeted instead by verbal jibes and threats painted on their fence, until their remarkable landlady becomes a catalyst for change. Beneath Joan's direct, deceptively simple narrative voice lies an emotionally complex tale. Drawing on his mother's immigrant experience as the basis for this moving story, Newbery Honor author Yep (*Dragonwings*; *The Rainbow People*) skillfully avoids pat or reductive explanations. He gives his heroine, for example, the maturity to recognize the biases her own family holds as well as the courage to stand up to the more blatant and violent prejudices of her neighbors. A traditional Chinese myth about the starfisher—half-bird, half-human, confined to the earth but yearning for the stars—weaves through the story, a poetic but insistent metaphor for Joan's own hopes and dreams. Ages 8–up.

Tongues of Jade
September 1991

Noted children's author Yep (*The Rainbow People*; *The Star Fisher*) scrupulously culls numerous early Chinese American tales, most of them collected as part of a 1930s WPA project in Oakland's Chinatown, and gracefully retells them, weaving everything together with perceptive commentary on the stories' origins and intents. Many of the virtues and morals espoused are from familiar folktale territory—the importance of respect for parents ("The Little Emperor") and of kindness to others ("Waters of Gold") and the pitfalls of greed ("The Rat in the Wall"). The stories are liberally dosed with magic, and all praise the qualities—patience and diligence, for example—necessary to succeed in a foreign and often hostile land. Kudos to Yep for preserving and interpreting these important historical links in the Chinese American experience.

List of Selected Works

Anthologies

The Rainbow People. New York: Harper & Row, 1989.

Tongues of Jade. New York: HarperCollins Children's Books, 1991.

Tree of Dreams: Ten Tales from the Garden of Night. Illustrated by Isadore Seltzer. Mahwah, NJ: Bridgewater, 1995.

Novels

The Amah. New York: G. P. Putnam & Sons, 1999.

Angelfish. New York: G. P. Putnam & Sons, 2001.

The Case of the Firecrackers: Chinatown Mystery #3. New York: HarperCollins Children's Books, 1999.

The Case of the Goblin Pearls: Chinatown Mystery #1. New York: HarperCollins Children's Books, 1997.

The Case of the Lion Dance: Chinatown Mystery #2. New York: HarperCollins Children's Books, 1998.

Child of the Owl. New York: Harper & Row, 1977.

Cockroach Cooties. New York: Hyperion Books for Children, 2000.

The Cook's Family. New York: G. P. Putnam & Sons, 1998.

The Curse of the Squirrel. Illustrated by Dirk Zimmer. New York: Random House, 1987.

Dragon Cauldron. New York: HarperCollins Children's Books, 1991.

Dragon of the Lost Sea. New York: Harper & Row, 1982.

Dragon's Gate. New York: HarperCollins Children's Books, 1993.

Dragon Steel. New York: Harper & Row, 1985.

Dragon War. New York: HarperCollins Children's Books, 1992.

Dragonwings. New York: Harper & Row, 1975.

Dream Soul. New York: HarperCollins Children's Books, 2000.

Hiroshima. New York: Scholastic, Inc., 1995.

The Imp That Ate My Homework. Illustrated by Benrei Huang. New York: HarperTrophy, 1998.

Kind Hearts and Gentle Monsters. New York: Harper & Row, 1982.

Lady of Ch'iao Kuo: Warrior of the South, Southern China, A.D. 531 (The Royal Diaries). New York: Scholastic, Inc., 2001.

Later, Gator. New York: Hyperion, 1995.

Liar, Liar. New York: William Morrow Books, 1983.

The Magic Paintbrush. Drawings by Suling Wang. New York: HarperCollins Children's Books, 2000.

The Mark Twain Murders. New York: Four Winds, 1982.

Monster Makers, Inc. New York: Arbor House, 1986.

Mountain Light. New York: Harper & Row, 1985.

My Name Is America: The Journal of Wong Ming-Chung—A Chinese Miner, California, 1852. New York: Scholastic, Inc., 2000.

The Red Warrior. New York: HarperCollins, 2005.

Ribbons. New York: G. P. Putnam & Sons, 1996.

Seademons. New York: Harper & Row, 1977.

Sea Glass. New York: Harper & Row, 1979.

The Serpent's Children. New York: Harper & Row, 1984.

Skunk Scout. New York: Hyperion Books for Children, 2003.

Spring Pearl: The Last Flower (Girls of Many Lands). Middleton, WI: Pleasant Company Publications, 2002.

The Star Fisher. New York: William Morrow Books, 1991.

Star Trek No. 22: Shadow Lord. New York: Pocket Books, 1985.

Sweetwater. Illustrated by Julia Noonan. New York: Harper & Row, 1973.

Thief of Hearts. New York: HarperCollins Children's Books, 1995.

The Tiger's Apprentice—The Tiger's Apprentice Book 1. New York: HarperCollins Children's Books, 2003.

The Tom Sawyer Fires. New York: William Morrow Books, 1984.

The Traitor. New York: HarperCollins Children's Books, 2003.

When the Circus Came to Town. Drawings by Suling Wang. New York: HarperCollins Children's Books, 2001.

List of Selected Awards

Child of the Owl **(1977)**
American Library Association Notable
   Book (1977)
Boston Globe/Horn Book Award for
   Fiction (1977)
New York Times Outstanding Books of the
   Year (1977)
School Library Journal Best Book (1977)

Dragonwings **(1975)**
American Library Association Notable
   Book (1975)
Boston Globe/Horn Book Award Honor
   Book (1977)

Children's Book Award, International Reading
   Association (1976)
Lewis Carroll Shelf Award (1979)
Newbery Honor Book (1975)
New York Public Library's Books for the Teen
   Age (1980, 1981, 1982)
New York Times Outstanding Book of the
   Year (1975)

***Dragon's Gate* (1993)**
Newbery Honor Book (1993)

***Dragon Steel* (1985)**
Child Study Association of America's Children's
   Books of the Year (1986)

***The Rainbow People* (1989)**
Boston Globe/Horn Book Honor Award (1989)

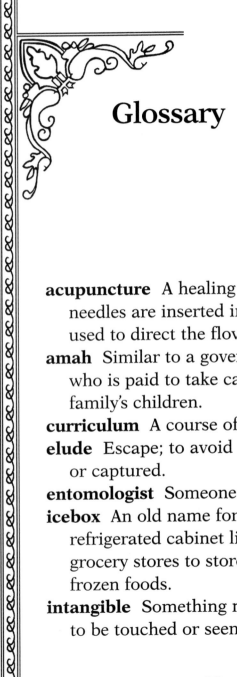

Glossary

acupuncture A healing practice in which needles are inserted into the body and used to direct the flow of energy.

amah Similar to a governess; a woman who is paid to take care of another family's children.

curriculum A course of study at school.

elude Escape; to avoid being caught or captured.

entomologist Someone who studies insects.

icebox An old name for a refrigerator or refrigerated cabinet like those used in grocery stores to store milk, soda, and frozen foods.

intangible Something not physical; unable to be touched or seen.

predecessors Those that came before, whether
books or people.

protagonist The primary character in a story,
book, or play.

PT boat Nicknamed "mosquito boats," these
were eighty-foot-long wooden boats that
carried a crew of twelve to fourteen, and
enough firepower to sink a battleship. PT
boats were used by the U.S. Navy in World
War II and the Vietnam War. The most
famous of these boats is the PT-109, which
was commanded by then Lieutenant John F.
Kennedy, who went on to become president
of the United States.

sestina A type of poem consisting of six stanzas
of six lines each, concluding with a three-line
stanza, all with a complex rhyme scheme.

skid row flophouse A place to sleep that
usually provides only beds and is used by
the very poor, including the homeless.

spring tonic Prior to modern medicine,
mothers, especially in rural areas, made
their children drink a "tonic" each spring.
The tonics were usually homemade, bitter
herbal drinks designed to wake the body
from the long winter. They often contained
large doses of vitamin C, so while they

tasted awful, they were actually good for the children.

tween A child between middle childhood and adolescence, usually between eight and twelve years old.

valor Courage or bravery; a quality that enables someone to face danger without running away.

For More Information

Web Sites

Due to the changing nature of Internet links, the Rosen Publishing Group, Inc., has developed on online list of Web sites related to the subject of this book. This site is updated regularly. Please use this link to access the list:

http://www.rosenlinks.com/lab/lyep

For Further Reading

"A Garden of Dragons." *The ALAN Review*,
Vol. 19, No. 3, Spring 1992, pp. 6–8.
"Attack of the Giant Teenage Space Dogs:
Notes of a Science Fiction Film Fan."
Top of the News, Vol. 39, No. 1, Fall
1982, pp. 92–94.
"Author's Commentary." *Children's Literature
Review*. Edited by Gerard J. Senick.
Detroit: Gale Research, Inc., 1989, Vol.
17, pp. 201–202.
"The Ethnic Writer as Alien." *Interracial
Books for Children Bulletin*, Vol. 10,
1979, p. 5.
"Fantasy and Reality." *Horn Book Magazine*,
Vol. 54, April 1978, p. 136.

"The Green Cord." *Horn Book Magazine*, Vol. 65, May–June 1989, pp. 318–322.

Kao, Karl S. Y. *Classical Chinese Tales of the Supernatural and the Fantastic*. Bloomington, IN: Indiana University Press, 1985.

Kraus, George. *High Road to Promontory: Building the Central Pacific Across the High Sierra*. Palo Alto, CA: American West Publishing Company, 1969.

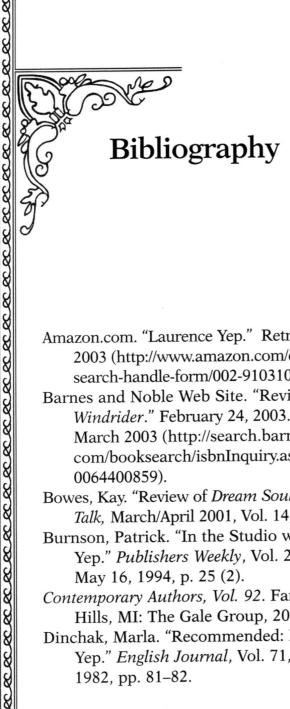

Bibliography

Amazon.com. "Laurence Yep." Retrieved January 2003 (http://www.amazon.com/exec/obidos/search-handle-form/002-9103100-2222443).

Barnes and Noble Web Site. "Review of *Windrider*." February 24, 2003. Retrieved March 2003 (http://search.barnesandnoble.com/booksearch/isbnInquiry.asp?isbn=0064400859).

Bowes, Kay. "Review of *Dream Soul*." *Library Talk*, March/April 2001, Vol. 14, Issue 2, p. 49.

Burnson, Patrick. "In the Studio with Laurence Yep." *Publishers Weekly*, Vol. 241, No. 20, May 16, 1994, p. 25 (2).

Contemporary Authors, Vol. 92. Farmington Hills, MI: The Gale Group, 2001.

Dinchak, Marla. "Recommended: Laurence Yep." *English Journal*, Vol. 71, No. 3, March 1982, pp. 81–82.

Fantastic Fiction. "Laurence Yep Biography." Retrieved February 2003 (http://www. fantasticfiction.co.uk/authors/Laurence_ Yep.htm).

Fisher, Margery. "Review of *Sweetwater* in *Growing Point*." Vol. 15, No. 6, December 1976, pp. 3012–3013. From *Contemporary Literary Criticism, Vol. 35*. Detroit: Gale Research Inc., 1985.

Gale Literary Databases. Contemporary Authors "Laurence Michael Yep." Farmington Hills, MI: The Gale Group, 2001. Volume 92, pp. 459–465.

Gendel, Adrienne, Maggie Hanley, and Kay E. Vandergrift. "Learning About Laurence Yep." Retrieved January 2003 (http://scils.rutgers.edu/ ~kvander/yep.html).

HarperCollins Children's Books Web Site. "Laurence Yep—Author Bio." Retrieved February 2003 (http://www.harpercollins.com/catalog/ author_xml.asp?authorID=12929).

HarperCollins Children's Books Web Site. "Read Our Interview with Laurence Yep and Jennifer Holm!" 2003. Retrieved March 2003 (http://www.harperchildrens.com/hch/author/ author/Tour/tour_int.asp).

HarperCollins Children's Books Web Site. "The Traitor: Golden Mountain Chronicles: 1885." 2003. Retrieved March 2003 (http://www. harperchildrens.com/catalog/book_interview _xml.asp?isbn=0060275227).

Haviland, Virginia. Review of *Child of the Owl*.
Horn Book Magazine, Vol. LIII, No. 4, August
1977, p. 447.

Johnson-Feelings, Dianne, and Catherine Lewis.
"Laurence Yep." *Writers for Young Adults*.
New York: Charles Scribner's Sons, 1997.

Lenhart, Maria. "Finding the Courage to Be
Oneself." *Christian Science Monitor*, October
15, 1979, p. B11.

Marcus, Leonard S. "Talking with Authors." *School
Library Journal*, Vol. 46, Issue 9, 2000, p. 50.

Marowski, Daniel G., ed. *Contemporary Literary
Criticism, Vol. 35.* Detroit: Gale Research
Inc., 1985.

Muller, Al. "Review of *Dragon of the Lost Sea*."
The ALAN Review, Vol. 10, No. 3, Spring
1983, p. 21.

Notable Asian Americans. "Laurence Yep."
Reproduced in Biography Resource Center.
Farmington Hills, MI: The Gale Group, 2003.
Retrieved January 2003 (http://www.galenet.
com/servlet/BioRC).

The Penguin Group Web Site. "Biography, Laurence
Yep." Retrieved March 2003 (http://www.
penguinputnam.com/Author/AuthorPage/
0,0000028405).

Public Broadcasting Corporation Web Site.
American Experience. "Transcontinental
Railroad." Retrieved February 2003
(http://www.pbs.org/wgbh/amex/tcrr).

"Review of *Seademons*." *Publisher's Weekly*, October 3, 1977, Vol. 212, No. 14, p. 94. From *Contemporary Literary Criticism, Vol. 35*. Detroit: Gale Research Inc., 1985.

Rooney, David. "Bagging 'Tiger' Trio." *Daily Variety*, March 23, 2003, p. 6.

Silvey, Anita, ed. *The Essential Guide to Children's Books and Their Creators*. New York: Houghton Mifflin Co., 2002.

Something About the Author, Vol. 123. Farmington Hills, MI: The Gale Group, 2001.

St. James Guide to Young Adult Writers, 2nd ed. St. James Press, 1999. "Laurence (Michael) Yep." Reproduced in Biography Resource Center. Farmington Hills, MI: The Gale Group. 2003. Document Number: K1663000474. Retrieved January 2003 (http://www.galenet.com/servlet/BioRC).

Tigard, Conan. "The Reading Nook Book Review. Review of *Shadow Lord*." Retrieved February 2003 (http://www.mtbca.com/shadowlord.html).

U.S. Department of Housing and Urban Development. "Celebrating Fair Housing." Retrieved March 2003 (http://www.hud.gov/offices/fheo/aboutfheo/history.cfm).

Yep, Laurence. *The Case of the Lion Dance: Chinese Mystery #2*. New York: HarperCollins, 1998.

Yep, Laurence. *Child of the Owl*. New York: HarperCollins Children's Books, 1977.

Yep, Laurence. *Cockroach Cooties*. New York: Hyperion Books for Kids, 2000.

Yep, Laurence. *Dragon's Gate*. New York: HarperCollins Children's Books, 1993.

Yep, Laurence. *Dream Soul*. New York: HarperCollins Children's Books, 2000.

Yep, Laurence. *The Lost Garden*. Englewood Cliffs, NJ: Julian Messner, 1991.

Yep, Laurence. *Tongues of Jade*. New York: HarperCollins Children's Books, 1991.

Source Notes

Introduction
1. Laurence Yep, *The Lost Garden* (New York: Simon & Schuster Books for Young Readers, 1991), p. 91.
2. Dinchak, Marla, "Recommended: Laurence Yep," *English Journal*, Vol. 71, No. 3, March 1982, pp. 81–82.

Chapter 1
1. Yep, *The Lost Garden* (New York: Simon & Schuster Books for Young Readers, 1991), p. 7.
2. Ibid., p. 9.
3. Ibid., p. 11.
4. Ibid., p. 12.
5. Ibid., pp. 13–14.
6. Ibid., p. 15.

7. Ibid., p. 23.
8. Ibid.
9. Ibid., p.38
10. Ibid., p. 45.
11. Ibid., p. 53.

Chapter 2

1. Laurence Yep, *The Lost Garden* (New York: Simon & Schuster Books for Young Readers, 1991), p. 77.
2. Ibid., p. 91.
3. Ibid.
4. Ibid., p. 93.
5. Ibid., p. 96.
6. Ibid., p. 99.

Chapter 3

1. Laurence Yep, *The Lost Garden* (New York: Simon & Schuster Books for Young Readers, 1991), p. 103.
2. Interview with Laurence Yep by Katherine Lawrence, March 2003.
3. Virginia Haviland, "review of *Child of the Owl*," *Horn Book Magazine*, Vol. LIII, No. 4, August 1977, p. 447.
4. "Laurence (Michael) Yep." *St. James Guide to Young Adult Writers*, 2nd ed., Detroit, MI: St. James Press, 1999. Reproduced in Biography Resource Center. Farmington Hills, MI: The Gale Group, 2003. Document number: K1663000474. Retrieved January 2003 (http://www.galenet.com/servlet/BioRC).

5. Al Muller. A review of "Dragon of the Lost Sea," *The ALAN Review*, Volume 10, No. 3, Spring 1983, p. 21.
6. Yep, *The Lost Garden*, pp. 105–106.
7. "Laurence Yep." The Penguin Group. Retrieved March 2003 (http://www.penguinputnam.com/ Author/AuthorPage/0,,0000028405).
8. Laurence Yep, *Dragon's Gate* (New York: HarperTrophy, 1993), front matter.
9. Yep, *The Lost Garden*, p. 31.

Chapter 4

1. Laurence Yep, *Dragon's Gate* (New York: HarperTrophy, 1993), front matter.
2. Laurence Yep, *The Lost Garden* (New York: Simon & Schuster Books for Young Readers, 1991), p. 60.
3. Yep, *Dragon's Gate*, p. 198.
4. HarperCollins Children's Books interview with Laurence Yep. *The Traitor* promotional tour, 2003.
5. Kay Bowes. *Library Talk*, March/April 2001, Vol. 14, Issue 2, p. 49.
6. Laurence Yep, *Dream Soul* (New York: HarperCollins Children's Books, 2000), preface.

Chapter 5

1. Interview with Laurence Yep by Katherine Lawrence, March 2003.
2. Laurence Yep, *Cockroach Cooties* (New York: Hyperion Books for Children, 2000), p. 3.
3. Yep, p. 5.
4. Yep, p. 135.

5. Laurence Yep, *The Case of the Lion Dance* (New York: HarperCollins Children's Books, 1998), p. 139.
6. Ibid.

Chapter 6

1. Notable Asian Americans. Reproduced in Biography Resource Center. Farmington Hills, MI: The Gale Group, 2003. Retrieved January 2003 (http://www.galenet.com/servlet/BioRC). Document number: K1620000242.
2. Leonard S. Marcus, "Song of Myself," *School Library Journal*, Vol. 46, Issue 9, September 2000, p. 50.
3. Notable Asian Americans.
4. Ibid.

Chapter 7

1. "Laurence Yep," *Authors and Artists for Young Adults*, Vol. 31. Gale Group, 2000. Reproduced in Biography Resource Center. Farmington Hills, MI: The Gale Group, 2003. Retrieved January 2003 (http:www.galenet.com/servlet/BioRC). Document number: K1603000577.
2. HarperChildrens.com, "Read Our Interview with Laurence Yep and Jennifer Holm!" 2003. Retrieved March 2003 (http://www.harperchildrens.com/hch/author/author/Tour/tour_int.asp).
3. Laurence Yep, *The Lost Garden* (New York: Simon & Schuster Books for Young Readers, 1991), p. 22.

4. HarperChildrens.com. *The Traitor* interview
   with Laurence Yep. 2003. Retrieved March
   2003 (http://www.harperchildrens.com/catalog/
   book_interview_xml.asp?isbn=0060275227).
5. Ibid.
6. Yep, pp. 21–22.
7. Ibid., p. 106.
8. Leonard S. Marcus, "Song of Myself," *School
   Library Journal*, Vol. 46, Issue 9, September
   2000, p. 50.

Index

About the Author

Katherine Lawrence has had more than thirty television scripts produced, most recently for *Stargate Infinity*, and was nominated for a Writers Guild of America Award in 1997. Other credits include writing computer games, short stories, and two nonfiction children's books, *Extreme Environments: Deserts* and a biography of actor/martial artist Jean-Claude Van Damme. Please visit her Web site at www.katherinelawrence.com.

Photo Credits

Cover and p. 2 Joanne Ryder.

Designer: Tahara Hasan; Editor: Annie Sommers